Interior Design in Japan

PAGE ONE PUBLISHING

Legend
Legende
Lègende

a: Title of Work
    Titel der Arbeit
    Titre du travail
b: Location
    Ort
    Location
c: Client
    Auftraggeber
    Client
d: Director / Planner
    Direktor / Planer
    Directeur / Planificateur
e: Designer / Agency
    Designer / Agentur
    Designer / Agence
f: Contractor
    Ausführendes Unternehmen
    Entreprise
g: Photographer
    Photograph
    Photographe
h: Comments
    Kommentar
    Observations
i: Main materials
    Wichtigste Materialien
    Matériaux principaux
j: Representative of the applicant
    Repräsentant der Agentur
    Représentant du demandeur
k: Administrator
    Leitung
    Administrateur

Works selected from
original titles "Interior Best Selection Vol. 1-5"
© 1984, 1986, 1988, 1990, 1992 by
Graphic - sha Publishing Co., Ltd.
First published in Japan by Graphic - sha Publishing Co., Ltd.,
Tokyo, Japan

© 1993 for this edition: Page One Publishing Pte., Ltd., Singapore
Distributed worldwide by
Könemann Verlagsgesellschaft mbH
Bonner Str. 126, D-50968 Köln

Designed by Peter Feierabend, Berlin
Typesetting: RZ-Werbeagentur, Hannover
Text: Rolf Toman, Esperaza
English translation: Michael Claridge, Bamberg
French translation: Thérèse Chatelain-Südkamp, Lohmar

Printed in Singapore
ISBN 981-00-4777-0

Contents

Inhalt

Sommaire

Foreword

Ninety per cent of all Japanese designers work for multicorporate enterprises. Their designs in the course of the past ten years have been the product of an ambitious collective effort, stemming from the desire to match the technological leap forward made in recent decades, and the well-known concomitant export figures, with an equally successful aesthetic mobilization, in order that the previously acquired share of the market be secured or further extended. The focus here has been on product design, in particular that of such goods as have been required to compete on the international market. It has been a question, in certain product areas, of finally closing the gap between the high reputation long enjoyed by Japanese brands from the technological viewpoint and the less satisfactory external appearance and finish of such products.

The international orientation of the expanding Japanese economy in general and product design in particular has not been without its effect on Japanese architecture and the sphere of interior design, the subject of this volume. This area has of course been confronted with problems of a quite different nature, primarily those of spatial economy, and to an extreme degree. Japan is a densely populated land, one, moreover, on which natural catastrophes are frequently visited. Tokyo, the Japanese capital and megametropolis, has had to be rebuilt twice this century, first of all in the aftermath of the great earthquake of 1923 and then following the destruction wrought by American bombs in the Second World War. The pressure to rebuild rapidly gave birth to an extraordinary dynamic. Growth in accordance with urban-development concepts, to say nothing of aesthetic notions, was totally out of the question. Today, Tokyo and the two neighbouring cities of Kawasaki and Yokohama, which it has meanwhile swallowed up, constitute a gigantic conglomeration. Embracing 32 million people within a radius of 50 kilometres, it is the largest conurbation in the world. It is virtually impossible to identify a centre of the giant city. "The urban centres move about," believes the architect Yoshinobu Ashihara, seeing this as related to the thoughtless willingness of the Japanese to accept constant change. "We are only too willing to cling to nowhere and nothing."[1]

Mobility – Flexibility – Multifunctionality: these are but three of the requirements to which architects – and particularly interior designers – in Japan must give special consideration, three aspects resulting from the imperative economy of space. In many locations, the scarcity of living space has led to prohibitively high prices, making it essential that both the – generally small – apartments and those commercial areas intended for offices, shops and restaurants be put to optimum use.

The precept of spatial economy lies at the base of the traditional style of Japanese home décor, with its *tatami* floors, low dining tables, and *shoji* sliding partitions, so admirably uncomplicated for the western observer and seemingly derived from the spirit of "noble Zen poverty"[2]. Mats served to divide up the area available in one room on its own or a few rooms together into functional zones for walking, sitting, eating, or sleeping, while the sliding paper partitions represented moveable borders between inside and outside, at once dividing up the room and letting in light, rendering curtains superfluous. Roland Barthes, the French author and sociologist, sees the sparse furnishings of the traditional Japanese house as also expressing a different idea of human living. In "L'Empire des Signes", his book on Japan, he writes: "For us, furniture has an immoveable quality, whereas the Japanese regard a house – a structure which will often be modified – as little more than a piece of furniture (...) the ideal Japanese house (...) contains not a single place that transmits the least sense of ownership, neither a sofa, nor a bed, nor a table, such as the body could utilize to construe itself as the subject (or master) of a room."[3] However one may choose to see this, the fact remains that the elementary virtues in design work – embodied in a restriction to that which is essential, in practicability, in functionality, in the craftsman's attention to detail, in a deep-seated understanding of natural materials such as stone, wood, bamboo, sisal – are shown to their best advantage in traditional interior design. What has become of these virtues?

With the exception of the two building materials of wood and stone – often used together, as in a wood and marble combination – the traditional materials of construction have been replaced by and large with modern ones, such as concrete, high-grade steel, corrugated iron, glass, plexiglass, ceramic tiles, and a variety of synthetic materials. It is quite possible to maintain quality in design when working with these, too, as has been illustrated by the work of Tadao Ando, the Japanese architect, and especially his housing projects, or that of the designers Shiro Kuramata and Shigero Uchida. They represent the perfect rendition of traditional Japanese design into a modern idiom. (Ando prefers to work with concrete, while Kuramata's favourite material was plexiglass.) It is characteristic of the quality inherent in their work that they dispense with superficial effects, hold up an aesthetic mirror to time through their reference to tradition, and are thus relatively timeless in the face of ever-changing fashion.

The problem facing Japanese designers in this respect is greater than anywhere else in the world. In no other industrialized country is the consumer society so bombarded with such a variety of products as in Japan. The producers test the marketability of a product directly, in terms of its reception by the customer, reacting in a highly flexible manner to whether it is accepted or rejected by the customer. In this way, the Japanese have learnt to become "co-producers", reacting correspondingly rapidly to trends in fashion. Even the "total-experience" areas created by the interior designers must ultimately hold their own as consumer goods. The number of visitors constitutes an important gauge of their degree of positive reception.

Spatial economy thus places ever greater requirements on multifunctionality, while the increased hunger for entertainment and the mania for the latest optical novelties make particular demands of the mobility and flexibility which interior design has to offer. These demands on the part of the public bring with them certain dangers if one is prepared to do them justice at any price through fashionable attitudes.

For decades, Japanese designers have primarily followed the model of western developments. The examples of recent house, restaurant and shop furnishings chosen for this volume similarly reveal an unmistakably western influence, as do the furnishings and fittings of industrial and public buildings cited here. Technical elements of function are left exposed and are incorporated into the spatial aesthetics; classical forms, such as columns, and other postmodern props are picked up again; works of sculpture – whether with or without any functional purpose – are created, such as give the rooms a particular, museum-like aura. On the other hand, the creations of Masaki Morita and those from the design offices of Kajima and Yamauchi/Aragaki also clearly attest to the fact that Japanese interior design shows itself at its best when it combines modern (western) elements with traditional (Japanese) ones. Masaki Morita speaks of a "re-Japanisation" of Japanese design. The signs are that people have been reflecting increasingly during the past few years on a rediscovery of cultural specifics.

This development, if it continues, can only be welcomed. The internationalization of markets tends to level out cultural differences. It is not only reasonable but also advisable to counteract this tendency – and not on aesthetic grounds alone. We well know the limits of monocultures now.

1   Quoted from Klaus Harpprecht: Oh Tokio. In: Merian, December 1992, p. 48
2   The expression stems from Walter Gropius, who used it in the foreword of a volume of photographs of the Katsura Palace, Yale University, 1960.
3   Roland Barthes: L'Empire des Signes, Paris 1981, p. 146

Vorwort

Neunzig Prozent der japanischen Designer sind Angestellte großer Konzerne. Was sie in den letzten zehn Jahren entworfen und gestaltet haben, ist das Ergebnis einer ehrgeizigen kollektiven Anstrengung. Der jahrzehntelangen technischen Aufrüstung mit den bekannten Exportresultaten sollte eine ebenso erfolgreiche ästhetische Mobilmachung an die Seite gestellt werden, um die erworbenen Marktanteile zu sichern oder noch zu erweitern. Im Mittelpunkt stand das Produktdesign, und zwar hauptsächlich der Güter, die sich auf internationalen Märkten zu behaupten hatten. Für einige Produktbereiche galt es, endlich die Lücke zu schließen zwischen dem Ruf, den japanische Fabrikate in technischer Hinsicht seit langem genießen, und der Wertschätzung ihres Outfits.

Die internationale Orientierung der expansiven japanischen Wirtschaft im allgemeinen und des Produktdesigns im besonderen blieb nicht ohne Auswirkung auf die japanische Architektur und den Bereich des Interieurdesigns, um den es in diesem Band geht. Allerdings waren und sind hier ganz andere Aufgaben zu lösen: raumökonomische hauptsächlich, und zwar extreme. Japan ist ein dicht besiedeltes und häufig von Katastrophen heimgesuchtes Land. Tokio, die japanische Hauptstadt und Megametropole, mußte in diesem Jahrhundert zweimal neu gebaut werden: nach dem großen Erdbeben von 1923 und nach den Zerstörungen des Zweiten Weltkriegs durch die Amerikaner. Der Zwang zum raschen Neuaufbau erzeugte eine außerordentliche Dynamik. Ein städtebaulich planmäßiges, gar ästhetischen Konzepten folgendes Wachstum war schier unmöglich. Tokio und die von ihr verschlungenen Nachbarstädte Kawasaki und Yokohama bilden heute ein gigantisches Konglomerat. Mit 32 Millionen Menschen in einem Radius von 50 Kilometern ist es das größte Ballungsgebiet der Welt. Ein Zentrum der Riesenstadt ist kaum auszumachen. „Die städtischen Zentren wandern", meint der Architekt Yoshinobu Ashihara und sieht dies im Zusammenhang mit der rücksichtslosen Bereitschaft der Japaner zur permanenten Veränderung: „Wir halten uns nirgendwo und an nichts allzusehr fest."[1]

Mobilität, Flexibilität, Multifunktionalität – das sind einige der Bedingungen, denen die Architektur und das Interieurdesign in Japan im besonderen Maß Rechnung zu tragen haben. Sie hängen mit der erzwungenen Raumökonomie zusammen. Der knappe Raum ist vielerorts unbezahlbar teuer geworden, also müssen die meist kleinen Wohnungen, müssen die gewerblichen Flächen für Büros, Läden und Restaurants optimal genutzt werden.

Schon die traditionelle Wohnkultur mit ihren Tatami-Böden, ihren niedrigen Eßtischen und Shoji-Schiebewänden, die dem westlichen Betrachter so bewundernswert klar und ganz dem Geist der „edlen Zen-Armut"[2] verpflichtet erscheint, basierte auf dem Gebot der Raumökonomie. Der durch Matten in Felder eingeteilte Boden eines einzigen oder weniger Räume diente Funktionen wie dem Gehen, Sitzen, Essen, Schlafen; und die verschiebbaren Papierwände waren bewegliche Grenze zwischen Innen und Außen, Raumteiler und Lichtdurchlaß, die einen Vorhang erübrigten. Für den französischen Schriftsteller und Soziologen Roland Barthes drückt sich in der Kargheit des – traditionellen – japanischen Hauses auch ein anderes menschliches Selbstverständnis aus. In seinem Japan-Buch „Das Reich der Zeichen" schreibt er: „Bei uns hat das Möbel eine immobile Bestimmung, während in Japan das Haus, das oft umgebaut wird, kaum mehr als ein Möbelstück ist (…) im japanischen Idealhaus (…) gibt es keinen Ort, der auch nur das geringste Eigentum bezeichnete: weder Sessel noch Bett noch Tisch, von denen aus der Körper sich als Subjekt (oder Herr) eines Raumes konstituieren könnte."[3] – Wie auch immer dies gesehen werden mag: Die Beschränkung auf das Notwendige, Praktikabilität, Funktionalität, handwerkliche Sorgfalt im Detail und ein tiefes Verständnis für natürliche Stoffe wie Steine, Holz, Bambus, Sisal sind die elementaren Designtugenden, die im traditionellen Interieurdesign zur Geltung kommen. Was ist aus diesen Tugenden geworden?

Abgesehen von den Baustoffen Holz und Stein, die häufig in Kombination (z.B. Holz und Marmor) verwendet werden, sind die traditionellen Baustoffe weitgehend von modernen wie Beton, Edelstahl, Wellblech, Glas, Plexiglas, Keramikfliesen und diversen Kunststoffen abgelöst worden. Auch an diesen kann sich Designqualität bewähren, wie die Arbeiten des japanischen Architekten Tadao Ando, vor allem seine Wohnhaus-Projekte, oder der Designer Shiro Kuramata und Shigero Uchida bezeugen. Sie stehen für die perfekte Umsetzung traditionellen japanischen Designs in eine moderne Sprache. (Ando arbeitet bevorzugt mit Beton, Kuramatas Lieblingsmaterial war Plexiglas.) Ein Qualitätsmerkmal ihrer Arbeiten liegt darin, daß sie auf vordergründige Effekte verzichten, daß sie durch ihren Bezug auf die Tradition Zeit ästhetisch reflektieren und somit resistent sind gegen schnellen modischen Verschleiß.

Das Problem, das sich japanischen Designern in dieser Hinsicht stellt, ist größer als irgendwo sonst auf der Welt. In keinem anderen Industrieland wird die Konsumgesellschaft mit einer solchen Produktvielfalt bombardiert wie in Japan. Die Produzenten „testen" die Verwendungsfähigkeit eines Produkts unmittelbar an der Akzeptanz des Kunden und reagieren sehr flexibel auf dessen Zuspruch oder Verweigerung. Die Japaner wurden auf diese Weise zum „Mitproduzenten" erzogen und reagieren entsprechend stark auf modische Trends. Auch die von den Interieurdesignern gestalteten „Erlebnis"räume haben sich letztlich wie Konsumprodukte zu bewähren. Die Besucherfrequenz ist dabei ein wichtiger Gradmesser für Akzeptanz.

Stellt also die Raumökonomie erhöhte Anforderungen an die Multifunktionalität, so gehen von dem gewachsenen Unterhaltungsbedürfnis und der Sucht nach immer neuen optischen Reizen besondere Ansprüche an die Mobilität und Flexibilität des Interieurdesigns aus. Solche Ansprüche des Publikums bergen gewisse Risiken, ihnen durch modische Attitüden um jeden Preis gerecht werden zu wollen.

Jahrzehntelang waren japanische Designer hauptsächlich an westlichen Entwicklungen orientiert. Auch die in diesem Band ausgewählten Beispiele neuerer Wohnungs-, Restaurant- und Ladeneinrichtungen sowie die Einrichtungen von Industrie- und öffentlichen Bauten zeigen unverkennbar westliche Einflüsse: Man läßt technische Funktionselemente unverkleidet und bezieht sie in die Raumästhetik ein, greift auf klassische Formen wie Säulen und andere postmoderne Versatzstücke zurück, schafft Skulpturen, mit oder ohne Gebrauchsfunktion, die den Räumen eine besondere, museale Aura geben. Die Gestaltungen von Masaki Morita, des Kajima- sowie der Yamauchi/Aragaki-Designbüros sind aber auch ein deutlicher Beleg dafür, daß das japanische Interieurdesign seine stärksten Seiten zeigt, wenn es moderne (westliche) mit traditionellen (japanischen) Elementen verbindet. Masaki Morita spricht von einer „Re-Japanisierung" des japanischen Designs. Es hat den Anschein, als besinne man sich in den letzten Jahren verstärkt auf die Wiederentdeckung der kulturellen Eigenheiten.

Diese Entwicklung, wenn sie sich denn fortsetzt, ist nur zu begrüßen. Die Internationalisierung der Märkte hat die Tendenz, kulturelle Differenzen einzuebnen. Dem entgegenzuwirken ist vernünftig und ratsam – nicht nur aus ästhetischen Gründen. Man weiß heute, was man von Monokulturen zu halten hat.

1   Zit. nach Klaus Harpprecht: Oh Tokio. In: Merian, Dez. 92, S. 48.
2   Der Ausdruck stammt von Walter Gropius; er gebraucht ihn im Vorwort eines Fotobandes über den Katsura-Palast, Yale University, 1960
3   Roland Barthes: Das Reich der Zeichen, Frankfurt a. M. 1981, S. 148 f.

Préface

Quatre-vingt-dix pour cent de tous les designers japonais travaillent dans un grand consortium. Leurs conceptions et réalisations de ces dix dernières années sont le fruit d'un effort collectif et ambitieux. Il était impératif d'accompagner la course à la technique, course qui dura plusieurs décennies et donna lieu aux succès que l'on sait dans l'exportation, d'une mobilisation esthétique tout aussi réussie si l'on voulait préserver ou même accroître les parts du marché que l'on venait d'acquérir. La place d'honneur fut accordée au design des produits, en particulier des marchandises qui devaient se ménager une place sur les marchés internationaux. Pour certains produits, il s'agissait de combler enfin les lacunes entre la réputation dont jouissaient depuis longtemps les fabrications japonaises sur le plan technique et l'estime à l'égard de leur apparence extérieure. L'orientation internationale de l'économie japonaise en général et du design du produit en particulier eut bien sûr des répercussions sur l'architecture japonaise et le domaine du design d'intérieur, lequel constitue le propos de ce livre. Toutefois, les problèmes à résoudre étaient – et sont – d'une tout autre nature: ils concernent l'utilisation de l'espace, et ce au plus haut point. Pays à forte densité de population, le Japon a été souvent victime de catastrophes. Durant ce siècle, Tokyo, capitale et mégalopole, a dû être reconstruite deux fois: après le terrible tremblement de terre de 1923 et après les destructions de la Seconde Guerre mondiale par les Américains. La nécessité d'une reconstruction rapide engendra une dynamique exceptionnelle. Une croissance urbaine planifiée ou obéissant seulement à des concepts esthétiques était tout à fait impossible. Tokyo et sa banlieue, à savoir les villes voisines Kawasaki et Yokohama, forment aujourd'hui un conglomérat gigantesque. Avec 32 millions de personnes sur un rayon de 50 kilomètres, cette région a la concentration industrielle et démographique la plus forte dans le monde entier. On peut à peine distinguer un centre dans cette ville gigantesque. «Les centres urbains se déplacent» affirme l'architecte Yoshinobu Ashihara qui voit dans ceci un rapport avec la mentalité des Japonais à accepter un changement en permanence: «Nous ne nous attachons jamais trop à un endroit ni à quelque chose.»[1]

Mobilité, flexibilité, multifonctionnalité – voici quelques-unes des conditions dont l'architecture et le design d'intérieur japonais durent tenir compte à un haut degré. Elles sont liées à cette économie forcée de l'espace. Dans beaucoup d'endroits, l'espace est si restreint qu'il est devenu hors de prix. Il faut donc aménager d'une façon optimale les appartements, petits pour la plupart, de même que les locaux pour les bureaux, les magasins et les restaurants.

La culture traditionnelle de l'habitat avec ses sols de tatami, ses tables basses et ses parois mobiles Shoji, qui aux yeux admirateurs des Occidentaux semble dominée par l'esprit de la «noble pauvreté Zen»[2], avait déjà pour commandement une utilisation optimale de l'espace. Divisé en plusieurs parties à l'aide de nattes, le sol d'une seule pièce ou d'un petit nombre de pièces permettait l'accomplissement de diverses fonctions comme marcher, s'asseoir, manger et dormir; quant aux parois mobiles en papier, elles servaient de frontière entre l'intérieur et l'extérieur, faisaient office de paravent et rendaient superflue l'utilisation d'un rideau en laissant passer la lumière. Pour l'écrivain et sociologue Roland Barthes, une conception différente du moi s'exprime dans le dépouillement de la maison japonaise traditionnelle. Dans son livre sur le Japon «L'Empire des Signes», il écrit: «Chez nous, le meuble a une vocation immobilière, alors qu'au Japon, la maison, souvent: reconstruite, est à peine plus qu'un élément mobilier (…) dans l'idéale maison japonaise (…) il n'y a aucun lieu qui désigne la moindre propriété: ni siège, ni lit, ni table d'où le corps puisse se constituer en sujet (ou maître) d'un espace.»[3] Quelle que soit la façon de voir, le fait de se limiter au nécessaire, à ce qui est praticable et fonctionnel, le soin apporté au détail dans le travail manuel ainsi qu'une compréhension profonde des matériaux comme la pierre, le bois, le bambou et le sisal sont les vertus premières du design, vertus mises en valeur dans le design d'intérieur traditionnel. Qu'est-il advenu de ces vertus?

Mis à part le bois et la pierre, qui sont souvent combinés à d'autres matériaux (par exemple, le bois et le marbre), les matériaux de construction traditionnels ont été largement remplacés par d'autres plus modernes comme le béton, l'acier inoxydable, la tôle ondulée, le verre, le plexiglas, les carreaux de céramique et diverses matières synthétiques. Il n'empêche que la qualité dans le design peut être également obtenue avec ces matériaux comme en témoignent les travaux de l'architecte Tadao Ando, en particulier ses projets de maisons d'habitation, ou des designers Shiro Kuramata et Shigero Uchida. Ils sont la preuve que l'on peut transposer parfaitement le design japonais traditionnel dans un langage moderne. (Ando travaille de préférence avec le béton et le matériau préféré de Kuramata était le plexiglas). Une caractéristique de la qualité de leurs travaux réside dans le fait qu'ils renoncent aux effets apparents, reflètent le temps d'une façon esthétique grâce aux références à la tradition et résistent par conséquent à l'usure rapide de la mode.

A ce sujet, le problème que rencontrent les designers japonais est plus important que n'importe où ailleurs. Dans aucun autre pays industriel, la société de consommation n'est confrontée à une si grande variété de produits. Les fabricants «testent» directement la capacité d'utilisation d'un produit suivant l'accueil que le client lui réserve et réagissent avec beaucoup de flexibilité à son approbation ou à son refus. De cette façon, les Japonais ont fini par devenir des «cofabricants» et réagissent fortement aux tendances de la mode. Les salles d'«animation» des designers d'intérieur doivent elles aussi faire leurs preuves à l'instar des produits de consommation. Le nombre de visiteurs est en l'occurrence un thermomètre précieux indiquant l'accueil qu'elles rencontrent.

Si l'aménagement de l'espace exige beaucoup de la multifonctionnalité, le besoin d'animation, qui est devenu plus accru, et la recherche effrénée d'excitations optiques toujours nouvelles deviennent des défis pour la mobilité et la flexibilité du design d'intérieur. De telles exigences de la part du public renferment certains risques qui seraient de les satisfaire à tout prix en adoptant les attitudes en vogue.

Pendant des dizaines d'années, les designers japonais se sont orientés aux développements de l'Occident. Les exemples sélectionnés dans cet ouvrage, à savoir les tout nouveaux aménagements d'appartements, de restaurants et de magasins ainsi que ceux des usines et des bâtiments publics, révèlent très clairement les influences occidentales: on laisse les éléments de fonction sans revêtement et on les intègre à l'esthétique spatiale, on a recours aux formes classiques comme les colonnes et à d'autres décorations post-modernes, on crée des sculptures avec ou sans fonction utilitaire qui donnent aux pièces une aura particulière de musée. En revanche, les réalisations de Masaki Morita, de Kajima et du bureau d'études Yamauchi/Aragaki fournissent aussi la preuve que le design d'intérieur japonais excelle dans l'art d'associer les éléments modernes (occidentaux) aux éléments traditionnels (japonais). Masaki Morita parle de «re-japonisation» du design japonais. Il semble que l'on réfléchisse de plus en plus ces dernières années sur la redécouverte des particularités traditionnelles.

On ne peut que se réjouir d'une telle évolution – si elle se poursuit. L'internationalisation des marchés a tendance à niveler les différences culturelles. S'y opposer est une tâche sage et judicieuse – et pas seulement pour des raisons esthétiques. On sait aujourd'hui ce que donnent les monocultures.

1   Cité d'après Klaus Harpprecht: Oh Tokio. In : Merian, décembre 1992, p. 48
2   L'expression est de Walter Gropius; il l'utilise dans la préface d'un album sur le palais Katsura, Yale University, 1960
3   Roland Barthes: L'Empire des Signes, Paris 1981, p.146

a: **Himeji City Hall-Andone**
b: Himeji-shi, Hyogo
c: Himeji City
d: Yutaka Ikemoto
   (Showa Sekkei Inc.)
f: Kumagai-gumi & Miki-gumi J.V.
g: SS. OSAKA
h: An ancillary facility integrated into the City Administration Building. It includes a room for special guests and an arbour in the roof garden.

   Anbau des Rathauses mit einem Raum für Ehrengäste und einem Baum auf der Terrasse.

Une annexe intégrée dans l'Hôtel de ville, comprenant une chambre pour des invités d'honneur et un arbre sur le toit en terrasse.

i: Walls: sen veneer dyed grey
   Floor: carpet / Arbour: metal

   Wände: graues Sen-Furnier
   Boden: Teppich / Baum: Metall

   Murs: Sen gris / Sol: tapis
   Arbre: métal

j: Showa Sekkei Inc.

a: **Uosho "Gimpei" Sannomiya**
b: Kobe - shi, Hyogo
c: Hiroshi Yukawa
d: Tanishita Architectural Office, Kichihei Tanishita
e: Tanishita Architectural Office, Kichihei Tanishita
f: Yuniho Co., Ltd.: Isao Kawanishi
g: Masaski Fukumoto

i: Floor: white cedar / Walls: genuine Juraku plaster / Ceiling: pine (medium-straight grain) / Columns, beams: old timbers

   Boden: weißes Zedernholz / Wände: echter Juraku-Gips / Decke: Kiefer (mittelfeine, gradlinige Maserung) / Säulen, Balken: alte Hölzer

   Sol: cèdre blanc / Murs: plâtre de Juraku véritable / Plafond: pin (madrure droite à nervures moyennes) / Colonnes, poutres: bois ancien

j: Tanishita Architectural Office

h: A "Kaiseki" (Japanese tea lunch) restaurant specializing in cooking fish transported directly from the fishing grounds. A restaurant where the features of seafood cuisine are well reflected.

   Kaiseki Restaurant (für Tee und kleine Gerichte), das sich auf fangfrische Meeresfrüchte und Fischgerichte spezialisiert hat. Die Gestaltung des Restaurants spiegelt den Charakter der Küche wider.

   Un restaurant japonais «Kaiseki» (salon de thé japonais), où l'on sert des fruits de mer et des spécialités de poissons, directement transportés de l'endroit où ils ont été pêchés. L'architecture du restaurant reflète cette cuisine particulière.

a: **Japanese Restaurant Tsukiji "Koyama"**
b: Chuo-ku, Tokyo
c: Tane Koyama
e: Taisei Corporation: Michio Nishimura
f: Taisei Corporation
g: Hattori Studio
h: A Japanese restaurant which can also be used for receptions. Unusually quiet and very luxurious. Part of the design concept was to create space for amenities.

Japanisches Restaurant, auch geeignet für größere Gesellschaften. Außergewöhnlich ruhig und luxuriös. Komfort stand beim Design im Vordergrund.

Un restaurant japonais servant aussi de salle de réunion. Exceptionnellement calme et luxurieux. En concevant les plans, le décorateur a prêté la plus grande attention au confort.
j: Taisei Corporation

a: **LUZ**
b: Urawa-shi, Saitama
c: Cs´LAB Co., Ltd.
d: Director: Shinichiro Suzuki / Designer: Chieko Fujiwara
f: Tanseisha Co., Ltd.
g: Nacasa & Partners
h: The utilization of natural light creates a space in which we can feel at rest.

Tageslichteinfall sorgt für ein entspannendes Ambiente.

Une source de lumière naturelle fait de cet endroit un lieu de détente.
i: Floor: trowelled screed finish / Sculpture: polished stainless steel

Boden: gespachtelter Estrichboden / Objekt: polierter Edelstahl

Sol: chape étalé à la truelle / Sculpture: acier inoxydable poli
j: Tanseisha Co.,Ltd.

14

a: **Food & Beverage - Caballo**
b: Shibuya-ku, Tokyo
c: Taiwa Inc.
d: Director: Naohiko Sugita (Mik
   Planning Co., Ltd.) /
   Design Planning: Haruto Koji (Mik
   Planning Co., Ltd.) /
   Lighting Design: Haruki Kaito /
   Kitchen Design: Suntory Limited,
   New Restaurant Concept
   department
e: Kogei Co.,Ltd., Mik Planning
   Co., Ltd.
f: Hiroshi Kiuchi, Capa
g: A large beer restaurant taking the
   19th century European travelling
   fairground as its theme. The
   designer's aim was to create a
   large open space.

   Große Biergaststätte, für die der
   europäische Jahrmarkt des 19.
   Jahrhunderts Pate stand. Ziel des
   Architekten war es, Raum zu
   schaffen.

   Une grande brasserie, dont le
   décor s'inspire des foires
   itinérantes du XIXe siècle en
   Europe. Le but du décorateur était
   de créer un endroit spacieux.
h: Fairground: PVC tiles /
   Walls: PB 12 + AEP paint

   Jahrmarkt: PVC-Fliesen /
   Wände: PB 12 und AEP-Farben

   Champ de foire: carrelage en
   PVC / Murs: PB 12 et peinture AEP
i: Mik Planning Co., Ltd

b: Minato-ku, Tokyo
c: Akasaka Beikoku Co., Ltd.
d: YD Work Studio Inc.
e: YD Work Studio Inc.
   Tetsuo Tomita
f: Build Co., Ltd.
g: T. Nacása & Partners

h: Ground floor: Delicatessen (take-away service) / 1st floor: "Kaiseki" (Japanese tea lunch) restaurant / (Ground floor) Floor: granite tiles / Walls: Hosokawa stone tiles / Ceiling: plasterboard, base coat / EP painted furniture: cherry wood

Erdgeschoß: Feinkostgeschäft (Gerichte zum Mitnehmen) / 1. Stock: Kaiseki Restaurant für Tee und kleine Gerichte / (Erdgeschoß) Boden: Granit-fliesen / Wände: Hosokawa-Steinfliesen / Decke: Fasergips-platten, Unterputzschicht / Möbel: Kirschholz (EP-Farbe)

Rez-de-chaussée: épicerie fine (à emporter) / 1er étage: restaurant «Kaiseki» (salon de thé japonais) / (Rez-de-chaussée) sol: carrelage en pierre Hosokawa / Plafond: plaques de plâtre, enduit de base / Meubles: cerisier peint en EP

i: (1st floor) Floor: tiles, floor covering / Walls: tiles, plaster / Ceiling: plasterboard, base coat / EP painted furniture: coloured cypress wood, cherry wood

(1. Stock) Boden: Fliesen, Bodenbeläge / Wände: Fliesen, Gipsverputz / Decke: Faser-gipsplatten, Unterputzschicht / Möbel: gebeiztes Zypressenholz, Kirschholz (EP-Farbe)

(1er étage) sol: carrelage, revêtement / Murs: carrelage, plâtre / Plafond: plaque de plâtre, enduit de base / Meubles: cyprès teinté, cerisier peint en EP

a: **The 21 Curry**
b: Minato - ku, Tokyo
c: Katsutoshi Takada
e: Etsuyoshi Yamauchi,
   Yoshimi Aragaki
f: I.M.S. Co., Ltd.
g: Satoshi Asakawa
h: Challenge to low cost.
i: Douglas pine veneer / Douglas
   pine laminated timber / concrete
   blocks

   Douglasfichtenfurnier /
   Douglasfichten-Schichtholz /
   Betonblöcke

   Placage de douglas / Douglas
   lamellé / Blocs de Béton
j: Atelier NIRAI

a: **Japanese Restaurant
   "Sogetsu"**
b: Kusatsu - shi, Shiga
c: Shiga Kanko Kaihatsu Co., Ltd.
d: Iseki Co., Ltd.
e: Rieko Kobayashi (Iseki Co., Ltd.)
f: Hiroyoshi Deguchi (Iseki Co., Ltd.)
g: Hiroshi Uemonza (Unica, Inc.)
h: A traditional Japanese restaurant
   redesigned with a totally new
   arrangement. The theme is "the
   Japanese feel".

   Japanisches Restaurant, bei
   dem überlieferte Formen völlig neu
   interpretiert wurden. Das Motto
   lautet „Japanische Atmosphäre".

   Un vieux restaurant de tradition
   japonaise complèment redécoré.
   La devise est «l'atmosphère
   japonaise».
i: Floor: natural stone, tiles / Walls:
   sprayed resin gradation coatin

   Boden: Naturstein, Fliesen /
   Wände: Abstufungen durch
   Sprühharz

   Sol: pierre naturelle, carrelage
   Murs: revêtement en résine
   pulvérisée par couches
j: Iseki Co., Ltd.

a: **Kirin Lagar Fiesta**
b: Bunkyo-ku, Tokyo
c: Kirin Brewery Co., Ltd.
d: Producer: Syoro Kawazoe /
   Art Director: Toyohiko Yano /
   Interior Design: Haruki Kaitou /
   Creative Management:
   Junichi Nochi
f: Tanseisha Co., Ltd.
g: Jun Mitomi
h: Temporary beer restaurant with the
   theme "Spanish culture".

   Bierlokal, Thema: „Die spa-
   nische Kultur".

   Brasserie temporaire ayant pour
   thème «La culture espagnole».
i: TM truss structure, Canvas
j: Tanseisha Co., Ltd.

a: **Cielo**
b: Osaka-shi, Osaka
d: Takenaka Corporation
   (Takao Hayashi, Hiroshi
   Shimotsuma)
f: Takenaka Corporation
h: Social facility on the top floor for
   the employees´use as a tea room,
   dining room and lounge.

   Angestelltenbereich im Ober-
   geschoß, dient als Cafeteria,
   Kantine und Aufenthaltsraum.

   Au dernier étage, structure
   sociale destinée aux employés
   comme salon de thé, salle à
   manger et salle de réunion.
i: Floor: carpet / Walls: white oak
   finished with coloured lacquer /
   Ceiling: EP-II paint on FG board

   Boden: Teppich / Wände:
   weiße Eiche, überzogen mit
   farbigem Glanzlack / Decke: EP
   II Farbe auf FG-Palette

   Sol: tapis / Murs: chêne blanc
   en vernis brillant / Plafond:
   plaque de FG peinte en EP-II
j: Takenaka Corporation

a: **Cosmetic House Yamagishi**
b: Kanazawa - shi, Ishikawa
c: Yamagishi Cosmetic shop Co.,
Ltd.
d: Yukihiro Soma
e: Yukihiro Soma, Kazuyo Miyata
f: Murono Glass Co., Ltd.
g: Takahiro Nakai (Atelier Posi)
h: A proposal for a shop where
the idea is to abolish the con-
ventional interview case and
emphasize communication by
arranging a counselling counter in
the centre.

Entwurf eines Ladens. Durch
einen Beratungstresen in der Mitte
soll die traditionelle Verkaufs-
situation aufgehoben und statt
dessen die Kommunikation in den
Vordergrund gerückt werden.

Une suggestion de magasin,
qui, grâce au comptoir de
consultation au milieu, supprime
la situation de vente classique et
donne à la communication une
place centrale.

i: Floor: terrazzo tiles, wooden
tiles / Walls and ceiling:
boarding, VP paint

Boden: Terrazzo- und Holz-
fliesen / Wände und Decke:
Täfelung und VP-Farbe

Sol: carrelage terazzo,
parquet / Murs et plafond:
lambrissage peint en VP.
j: Wit Design Company

a: **Res Nova 21**
b: Osaka - shi, Osaka
c: Kinoshita Co., Ltd.
d: Etsuo Yamada, Kazumi
   Hayakawa
f: Matsushita IMP Co., Ltd.

g: Hitoshi Kawamoto
h: Showroom and shopping
   functions are united by
   creating diverse spaces with a
   variety of different wall surfaces.

   Unterschiedliche Wandober-
   flächen gliedern den Raum in
   verschiedene Bereiche für Vor-
   führung und Verkauf.

   Les différents revêtements
   muraux divisent la pièce en
   plusieurs espaces pour la
   présentation et la vente.

i: Floor: marble, carpet / Ceiling:
   paint and mosaic tiles

   Boden: Marmor, Teppich /
   Decke: Farbe und Mosaikfliesen

   Sol: marbre, tapis / Plafond:
   peinture et mosaïque
j: PC Design Office Co., Ltd.

a. **Department Store Senndai Vivre**
b: Sendai - shi, Miyagi
c: DAC City Sendai Vivre Co., Ltd
d: Art Director: Momo Commercial, Tae - Young Lee / Designer: Nomura Co., Ltd., Yuji Hirata, Cinq Art Co., Ltd., Hiroshi Kono
f: Nomura Co., Ltd.
g: Kenichi Suzuki

h: An entrance area that attempts to symbolize "modern times" with mirrors as an element which transcends reality and fantasy.

Eingangshalle, deren Spiegel als ein Element, das Realität und Vorstellungswelt überschreitet, sollen die modernen Zeiten symbolisieren.

Un magasin spécialisé dans les tenues de loisirs importées pour les jeunes gens. La décoration d'intérieur est mise en valeur par les murs irréguliers et blancs en plâtre.

i: Plaster, flooring, deformed bars, granite

Kalkputz, Boden, verformte Träger, Granit

Plâtre, sol, barreaux déformés, granit

j: Zeniya, Inc.

a: **Studio Ask Machida**
b: Setagaya - ku, Tokyo
c: Studio Ask, Inc.
d: Hiromitsu Mizuno (D'urban)
e: Kenji Shinozaki, Noriki Yamagami (Zeniya, Inc.)
f: Zeniya, Inc.
g: New Photo Studio
h: This is a store specializing in imported casual clothes for young people. The effect of space is enhanced by the uneven white plastered walls.

Ein Geschäft, das importierte Freizeitkleidung für junge Leute anbietet. Die Wirkung der Raumgestaltung wird durch den unregelmäßigen, weißen Putz der Wände verstärkt.

Un hall d'entrée qui tend à symboliser «Les temps modernes» avec des miroirs, élément dépassant la réalité et l'imagination.

i: Mortar base covered with leather, glass, tiles, sand spray, artificial rock facing, special paint

Mörtelunterlage mit Glasstücken, Fliesen, Sandspray, künstlicher Steinschicht und Spezialfarbe überzogen

Base en mortier, recouvert de cuir, de verre, de carrelage, sable pulvérisé, revêtement en pierre artificielle, peinture spéciale

j: Nomura Co., Ltd.

a: **Inoue Sacs One · Oh · Nine**
b: Shibuya - ku, Tokyo
c: Inoue Corporation
d: Masaki Morita
e: Masaki Morita
f: Nap International
g: Hiroyuki Hirai / Takeshi Nakasa
i: Floor: marble (coloured sand
   finish) / Walls: AEP paint /
   Cone: aluminium

   Boden: Marmor (Sandfarben) /
   Wände: AEP / Kegel: Aluminium

   Sol: marbre (couleur sable) /
   Murs: peinture AEP / Cône:
   aluminium
j: Design. M: Masaki Morita
k: Nap International

a: **Boutique Kuro**
b: Osaka - shi, Osaka
c: Mariko Hayase
e: Takenaka Corporation
   (Takao Hayashi; Kayoko Kanai)
f: Takenaka Corporation
g: Hiraku Shono

h: A very tense and rigid atmosphere
   is softened by the texture of the
   walnut counter.

   Die spannungsreiche und
   strenge Atmosphäre wird durch
   die Maserung des Ladentisches
   aus Walnußholz aufgelockert.

   L'atmosphère très tendue et
   sévère est adoucie par la
   madrure du guichet en noyer.

i: Floor: marble / Walls and
   columns: black granite / Ceiling:
   painted

   Boden: Marmor / Wände
   und Säulen: schwarzer Granit /
   Decke: Farbe

   Sol: marbre / Murs et
   colonnes: granit noir / Plafond:
   peint
j: Takenaka Corporation

a: **Diva et Diva**
b: Shibuya - ku, Tokyo
c: Ihiju Corporation
d: Masaki Morita
e: Masaki Morita
f: Nap International
g: Takeshi Nakasa
j: Design. M: Masaki Morita
k: Nap International

a: **Un**
b: Takasaki - shi, Gunma
c: Un Justice Co., Ltd.
e: Yoshiaki Ishii
f: Watanabe Co., Ltd.
g: Masahiro Tomita

a: **Inoue Sacs Yokosuka**
b: Yokosuka - shi, Kanagawa
c: Inoue Corporation
d: Masaki Morita
e: Masaki Morita
f: Hakusui Sha
g: Takeshi Nakasa
i: Floor: coloured concrete with
   terazzo insets / Walls: AEP
   paint / Pillar: Sigmult paint

   Boden: Beton mit Terrazzo /
   Wände: AEP - Farbe / Pfeiler:
   Sigmult-Farbe

   Sol: béton recouvert de
   terrazzo / Murs: peinture AEP /
   Pilier: peinture Sigmult
j: Design. M: Masaki Morita
k: Hakusui Sha

a: **Narcissus**
b: Kobe - shi, Hyogo
c: Noriko Yamamoto
e: Urban Gauss: Toshiroh Ikegami,
   Hirokazu Morii
f: Yamane Komuten
g: Yoshiharu Hata
h: The building has a light purple
   relief which marks the starting
   point of the town landscape. The
   angled mirrors create an internal
   spaciousness.

   Ein hellviolettes Relief macht das
   Gebäude zu einem eindrucks-
   vollen Punkt im Stadtbild. In den
   Ecken angebrachte Spiegel
   erzeugen einen Eindruck von
   Weite.

   Un relief violet clair fait du
   bâtiment un point marquant dans
   le paysage urbain. Des miroirs
   posés en angles donnent une
   impression d'espace.

i: Floor: coloured concrete / Walls
   and ceiling: VP paint / Furniture:
   tubular stainless steel, glass
   shelves

   Boden: farbiger Beton /
   Wände und Decke: VP-Farbe /
   Möbel: Glasregale mit Edel-
   stahlröhren.

   Sol: béton coloré / Murs et
   plafond: peinture VP / Meubles:
   étagères en verre avec des tubes
   en acier inoxydable.

j: Toshiroh Ikegami

Matsuda
26 Bd. Raspail, 75007 Paris
Nicole Co., Ltd.
YD Work Studio:
Ryoichi Yokota, Junji Koshiba
STC Christian Tourneroche
S.A.R.L.
T. Nacása & Partners
"MATSUDA" is the overseas
brand name of Nicole. This shop
is the first outlet in Paris following
those in Hong Kong, Singapore,
and New York. An image of
openness has been created in the
shop in Paris where many stores
express a rather introverted mood.
Although consideration was given
to this situation, the project
attempted to create a design
which does not deviate from the
basic store design philosophy of
Nicole.

Pariser Filiale für „MATSUDA" -
Produkte, dem ausländischen
Markenzeichen von Nicole.
Dieser Laden wurde im Anschluß
an die Filialen in Hong Kong,
Singapur und New York eröffnet.
Die Innenarchitektur zeichnet sich
durch eine großzügige Gestaltung
des Verkaufsraumes aus, um sich
von der Enge anderer Mode-
geschäfte in Paris abzugrenzen;
dennoch hat man versucht, ein
Design zu verwirklichen, das den
Grundsätzen für die Gestaltung
der „Nicole"- Läden entspricht.

Filiale parisienne pour les
produits «MATSUDA», la marque
de fabrique de Nicole à
l'étranger.Ce magasin a été
ouvert juste après les filiales de
Hong Kong, Singapour et New
York. La décoration d'intérieur se
caractérise par une décoration
spacieuse pour se démarquer des
autres magasins de mode géné-
ralement étroits. Cependant, le
design adopté correspond dans
sa base à la philosophie de
Nicole.

i: Floor: marble, Japanese oak
flooring / Walls: Japanese oak
pillars, stained Japanese oak
hanging panels / Display: stage
marble

Boden: Marmor, japanische
Eiche / Wände: Pfeiler aus
japanischer Eiche, Vertäfelung
aus gebeizter japanischer Eiche /
Vorführbühne aus Marmor

Sol: marbre, chêne japonais /
Murs: piliers en chêne japonais,
lambrissage en chêne japonais
teint / Scène de présentation en
marbre

j: YD Work Studio

a: **Ice Grey**
b: Shibuya - ku, Tokyo
c: Batsu Co., Ltd.
e: Design. M: Masaki Morita
f: Hakusuisha Co., Ltd.
g: T. Nacása & Partners, Hiroyuki Hirai
h: The aim of the project was to upgrade a video rental shop. The design concept attempts to create the sensation of a boutique.

Durch die Gestaltung nach dem Vorbild einer Boutique erhält diese Videothek ein höherwertiges Image.

Grâce à la reprise du décor d'une boutique, cette vidéotheque a amélioré son image.
i: Steel mesh, polyethylene, plywood, VP paint

Maschenmatte aus Stahl, Polyethylen, Sperrholz, VP-Farbe

Natte avec des mailles en acier, polyéthylène, contreplaqué, peinture VP
j: Design. M: Masaki Morita

a: **Nanba City Creators -
Renewal**
b: Osaka - shi, Osaka
c: Nankai Electric Railway
d: Art director: Takenaka
Corporation, Hisao Kiya
(Nomura Co., Ltd) Designer:
Toshiyuki Taya, Kaoru Takeuchi
(Nomura Co., Ltd)
f: Takenaka Corporation Nomura
Co., Ltd.
h: Design based on the concept of
a "creators museum".

Die Raumgestalter haben mit
diesem Entwurf ihr eigenes
Museum geschaffen.

Les décorateurs ont créé avec
ce projet leur propre musée.
i: Ceiling: PB ground with EP
finish / Floor and colums: marble

Decke: PB - Untergrund mit EP-
Anstrich / Boden und Säulen:
Marmor

Plafond: base en PB avec de la
peinture EP / Sol et colonnes:
marbre

a: **In and Out**
b: Minato - ku, Tokyo
c: Isao Ohnishi
d: Masaki Morita
e: Masaki Morita
f: Nap International
g: Takeshi Nakasa
j: Design. M: Masaki Morita
k: Nap International

Antique Potter Heian
Chiyoda - ku, Tokyo
Antique Potter Heian
Teiichi Nishikawa
Kajima Corporation
KK Kawasumi Architectural
Photograph Office
An antique dealer, located on the
ground floor of a tenant building
with tables and stools for tea
ceremonies. The business mainly
deals in Bizenware of the Heian
and Muromachi periods.

Antiquitätengeschäft im Erdgeschoß eines Mietshauses mit
Tischen und Sitzgelegenheiten für
Teezeremonien. Hier werden
hauptsächlich stücke aus der
Heian- und Muromachi-Zeit
verkauft.

Un magasin d'antiquités, au
rez-de-chaussée d'un bâtiment
habité, avec des tables et des
tabourets pour les cérémonies du
thé. Principalement, des pièces
des époques Heian et Muromachi
sont vendues.

i: Genuine Juraku plaster, silver foil,
     carpet, Japanese lacquer,
     imported granite, Tatami mats

     Echter Juraku Gips, Silberfolie,
     Teppich, japanische Lackfarbe,
     importierter Granit, Tatami-
     Matten (Stabmatten)

     Plâtre Juraku véritable, feuille
     d'argent, tapis, vernis japonais,
     granit importé, tatamis
j: KAJIMA DESIGN (Kajima
     Corporation Architectural and
     Engineering Design Group)

a: **Nikkei Shimbun Nankou Annex**
b: Osaka - shi, Osaka
c: Nihon Keizai Shimbun, Inc.
e: Tabenaka Corporation
   Masaya Inoue, Takashi
   Nakamoto Tomoaki Kawai
f: Takenaka Corporation
g: Katsuhiro Oshima
h: Both the exterior and interior of
   this new office building for the
   Nikkei Newspaper Inc. are
   designed as a new symbol for the
   company and as a centre for
   disseminating information in a
   high-tech context.

Architektur und Raumgestaltung
des neuen Geschäftsgebäudes
der Nikkei Newspaper Inc. reprä-
sentieren das Unternehmen und
bilden die Grundlage für eine
hochmoderne Nachrichtenüber-
mittlung.

L'architecture et la décoration
du nouvel immeuble de bureaux
de Nikkei Newspaper Inc. repré-
sente la companie et constitue la
base pour une transmission
d'information ultra-moderne.

i: Entrance hall: Floor: patterned
   ceramic tiles / Ceiling: sound-
   absorbing asbestos
   Exhibition hall: Floor: carpet tiles
   Walls: painted / Ceiling: painted
   plasterboard

   Eingangshalle: Boden: gemusterte
   Keramikfliesen / Decke: Schall-
   schluckendes Asbest
   Austellungshalle: Boden: Teppichfliesen / Wände: Farbanstrich /
   Decke: Gipsplatten mit Farbanstrich

   Hall d'entrée: Sol: céramique
   à motifs / Plafond: amiante pour
   amortir les bruits
   Hall d'eposition: sol: tapis /
   Murs: peinture / Plafond: plâtre
   peint
j: Takenaka Corporation

a: **Fujitsu oa Showroom Shinjuku**
b: Shinjuku - ku, Tokyo
c: Fujitsu Limited
d: GK Sekkei Associates
e: GK Sekkei Associates
f: Tanseisha Co., Ltd.
g: T. Nakasa & Partners
h: - A monolithic space is created in order to reflect competition with other companies and to captivate the attention of visitors.

Ein monolithischer Raum, der die Stellung des Unternehmens im Konkurrenzkampf symbolisieren und die Aufmerksamkeit des Besuchers auf sich ziehen soll.

Un endroit monolithique, reflètant la compétition avec d'autres entreprises et captant l'attention de visiteurs.

i: Steel products, punchings, metals, aluminium, granite

Stahl, Lochungen, Metalle, Aluminium, Granit

Acier, perforations, métaux, aluminium, granit
j: GK Sekkei Associates
k: Tanseisha Co., Ltd.

a: **Nishihonmachi Intes**
b: Osaka - shi, Osaka
c: Ko kaihatsu
d: Takenaka Corporation / Kiyoyuki Kadokawa, Hiroyuki Shimizu
g: Yukio Yoshimura, Taizo Furukawa
h: This building, with a fine balance between functionality, amenity and identity, was designed with "simplicity and closeness to nature"as its theme.

Unter dem Motto „Einfachheit und Naturverbundenheit" verbindet dieses Gebäude Funktionalität, Ästhetik und Individualität.

Sous le thème «simplicité et attachement à la nature», cet immeuble est synonyme de fonctionnalité, esthétique et individualité.

i: Floor and walls: marble (entrance hall) / Floor: carpet tiles (Offices)

Wände und Boden: Marmor (Eingangshalle) / Boden: Teppichfliesen

Sol et murs: (hall d'entrée): marbre / Sol: carrés de moquette

j: Takenaka Corporation
k: Takenaka Corporation

a: **Tokyo Kaijo Building**
b: Osaka - shi, Osaka
c: The Tokyo Kaijo Insurance Co., Ltd.
d: Director & Designer: Kunihide Oshinomi (KAJIMA DESIGN) / Designer: Yukishige Miyamae (KAJIMA DESIGN), Ryutaro Kazama, Midori Tando (ILYA Corporation)
f: Kajima Corporation, Osaka Branch
g: Yoshiteru Baba (Nacása & Partners)
h: As amenities are also necessary in a working environments the interior design aims at reflecting this concept.

Durch die Gestaltung des Arbeitsbereiches wurde eine angenehme Arbeitsatmosphäre geschaffen.

Une atmosphère agréable a été créée par la décoration de l'aire de travail.

i: Floor: marble, carpet, flooring / Walls: Sigmat plaster / Ceiling : polyurethane finish

Boden: Marmor, Teppich / Wände: „Sigmat-Gips" / Decke: Polyurethananstrich

Sol: marbre, tapis / Murs: plâtre, Sigmat / Plafond: peinture polyuréthanique

j: KAJIMA DESIGN (Kajima Corporation Architectural and Engineering Design Group)

a: **UCC Coffee Museum**
b: Kobe - shi, Hyogo
c: Ueshima Coffee Co., Ltd.
e: Takenaka Corporation / Fumio Nakahara, Akiko Matsushita
f: Takenaka Corporation
g: Yoshiharu Matsumura
h: The first coffee museum in the world, in which the coffee cup once built for the Portpia Faire of 1981 has been extended and reconstructed.

Das erste Kaffee-Museum der Welt mit einer vergrößerten Rekonstruktion der für die Portpia-Ausstellung von 1981 angefertigten Kaffeetasse.

Le premier musée du monde dans lequel se trouve une reproduction agrandie de la tasse à café faite en 1981 pour l'exposition de Portpia.

i: Atrium floor: black granite patterned flooring / Walls: Jolypate / Illuminated ceiling: enamelled steel panels

Boden des Innenhofs: schwarzer gemusterter Granit / Wände: „Jolypate" / Deckenbeleuchtung: emaillierte Stahltafeln

Sol de l'atrium: granit noir veiné/ Murs: «Jolypate» / Eclairage du plafond: plaques d'acier émaillées

j: Takenaka Corporation

a: **Spiral**
b: Minato - ku, Tokyo
c: Wacoal Corporation
e: Fumihiko Maki + Maki & Associates
f: Takenaka Komuten Co., Ltd
g: Toshiharu Kitajima
i: Floor: carpet / Walls: Yugoslavian marble / Ceiling: plasterboard, emulsion paint

Boden: Teppich / Wände: jugoslawischer Marmor / Decke: Gipsplatten, Emulsionsfarbe

Sol: tapis / Murs: marbre yougoslave / Plafond: plaque de plâtre, vernis-émulsion

j: Fumihiko Maki + Maki & Associates

a: **Ikuta Studio, Nippon Television Network Corporation**
b: Kawasaki - shi, Kanagawa
c: Nippon Television Network Corporation
d: Mitsubishi Estate Co., Ltd.
e: Kunihira Yamaguchi, Rokuro Hashimoto, Tetsuya Tsukada
f: Joint Venture of Taisei Corporation and Obayashi - Gumi Corporation
g: Koshi Miwa
h: This is one of the leading TV studios in Japan, noted for its drama productions. Because drama productions represent today's visual culture the basic theme of the design is a creative space.

Eines der führenden Fernsehstudios in Japan, bekannt für seine Theaterproduktionen. Das Design will Raum für Kreativität schaffen, da Theaterproduktionen gegenwärtige Fernsehkultur verkörpern.

Un des studios les plus importants au Japon, connu surtout pour ses productions de théâtre. Comme celles-ci représentent la culture visuelle d'aujourd'hui, l'objectif du design est de créer un espace créatif.

i: Exterior: gloss tiles (60 x 227 mm) / Glass: thermal control glass

Außenfläche: Glanzfliesen (60 x 227 mm) / Glasflächen: Wärmeschutzglas

Extérieur: carrelage brillant (60 x 227 mm) / Vitres: verre calorifuge
j: Interior Design and Proposal Section, Taisei Corporation

48

a: **Tokyo dec Parc**
b: Akikawa - shi, Tokyo
c: Digital Equipment Corporation
   Japan
d: Akihiko Hamada, Hideyuki
   Yamashita, Mikio
   Furusawa (Nikken Sekkei)
f: Kajima Corporation
g: Koji Horiuchi
h: By selecting simple and pure
   materials, a form has been
   established that enables the spac
   itself to appeal to our minds.

   Die Verwendung von einfachen
   und schlichten Materialien läßt
   den Raum für sich sprechen.

   Grâce à l'utilisation de matériaux simples et purs, l'espace
   laisse libre cours à notre
   imagination.
i: Lacquer finish and rubber tiles
   after Keikaru, plate, putty on
   fairfaced concrete

   Lackanstrich, Gummifliesen nach
   Keikaru, Blech, Kitt auf Sichtbeto

   Vernis, carrés en caoutchouc sur
   tôle Keikaru, mastic sur béton
   apparent
j: Nikken Sekkei

50

Toporo 51

Osaka - shi, Osaka

Takahashi - Building, Inc.

Mitsuro Nomura, Takahashi Matsuoka, Takenaka Corporation

Takenaka Corporation

Yoshiharu Natsumura

A random combination of geometric fragments containing a discordant, inherent flow, and speed, force and direction.

Willkürliche Zusammenstellung von geometrischen Formen, wodurch dem Design eine dissonante Note sowie Schwung, Ausdruckskraft und Richtung verliehen werden.

Le design donne une note dissonante ainsi qu´un mouvement, une forme d´expression et une direction grâce à une configuration arbitraire de formes géometriques.

Floor: carpet tiles / Walls: exposed concrete / Ceiling: exposed concrete

Boden: Teppichfliesen / Wände: Sichtbeton / Decke: Sichtbeton

Sol: carrés de tapis / Murs: béton apparent / Plafond: béton apparent

Takenaka Corporation

a: **Mr. Miyamoto´s house**
b: Suita - shi, Osaka
c: Takamitsu Miyamoto
d: Ichiyo Uta
f: Nakano Komuten
g: Yoshiharu Matsumura
h: Various effects are produced with lights, spaces, colours and forms.

Unterschiedliche Effekte durch Beleuchtung, räumliche Gestaltung, Farben und Formen.

Divers effets dûs à la luminosité, à la décoration de la pièce, aux couleurs et aux formes.

i: Floor: beechwood flooring / Walls: covered with cloth / Ceiling: covered with crumpled gold or silver paper

Boden: Buchenholz / Wände: Textiltapete / Decke: faltiges Gold- und Silberpapier

Sol: hêtre / Murs: tapisserie en tissu / Plafond: papier doré et argenté froissé

j: Ichiyo Uta Architect & Associates

a: **Mr. & Mrs. T Swimming House**
b: Nagoya - shi, Aichi
d: Miyagi Design Associates: Yukiko Miyagi
e: Yukiko Miyagi, Shingo Mito
f: Ohbayashi Gumi Ltd.
g: Center Photo
h: A building which can be used privately for sports such as swimming, athletics, etc. The interior decoration is laminated timber with a red cedar finish. The wooden building, matching the natural environment, imparts a rich sense of liberation.

Ein Gebäude, das sich für private sportliche Aktivitäten wie Schwimmen und Kraftsport nutzen läßt. Die Inneneinrichtung besteht aus Schichtholz mit rotgebeiztem Zederfurnier. Dieses Gebäude paßt sich an die natürliche Umgebung an und vermittelt ein Gefühl von Freiheit.

Un bâtiment pouvant servir à des activités sportives privées comme la natation ou l'athlétisme. La décoration d'intérieur est en cèdre stratifié. Ce bâtiment en bois est en harmonie avec l'environnement naturel et donne un sentiment de liberté.

i: Red cedar, Douglas pine, tiles, hanging cloth

Zederfurnier, Douglasfichte, Fliesen, Textiltapete

Contre-plaqué en cèdre, pin douglas, carrelage, tapisserie en tissu

j: Miyagi Design Associates

a: **Ichikawa Residence**
b: Ichikawa - shi, Chiba
c: Hideki Okada
d: Munehiko Taniguchi, Masahiro Nagumo
f: Yamazaki Komuten, Inc.
g: Shigeru Kaneko (Shigeru Kaneko Photo)
h: Considering the movement of the visual point from the staircase, we devised a mirror arrangement evoking a sense of change and breadth in the living room.

Von der Treppe aus sehen wir einen Spiegel, der das Gefühl von Weite im Wohnraum vermittelt.

En déplaçant notre regard de la cage d'escalier, l'effet miroir donne une impression de changement et de largeur à la salle de séjour.
i: Exterior walls: Ramada panelling / Interior: cloth / Floor: flooring, underfloor heating

Außenwände: Ramada-Verschalung / Innenwände: Textiltapete / Boden: Bodenbelag und Fußbodenheizung

Murs extérieurs: panneaux Ramada / Murs intérieurs: tapisserie en tissu / Sol: revêtement et sol chauffant
j: Kogakuin University Department of Architecture, Office of Taniguchi

a: **Tokyo Residence**
b: Midori - ku, Kanagawa
c: Hiroyuki Toko
d: Junji Kawada
f: Okura Kensetsu Co., Ltd.
g: Satoshi Asakawa
h: We have created a stimulating, but reserved space by combining natural elements on a base of exposed concrete.

Durch die Verwendung von natürlichen Baustoffen auf Sichtbeton ist eine entsprechende und gleichzeitig schlichte Raumgestaltung gelungen.

Grâce à l'utilisation de matériaux de construction naturels sur une base de béton, une décoration simple et appropriée a été créée.

i: Reinforced concrete, RC with paint finish, bricks, Douglas pine, plaster

Stahlbeton mit und ohne Farbanstrich, Mauersteine, Douglasfichte, Gips

j: Junichi Kawada Architect & Associates

a: **Takai Residence**
b: Nishinomiya - shi, Hyogo
c: Ryokichi Takai
e: Toshiroh Ikegami
f: Okura Shinko Co., Ltd.
g: Studio MAX: Yoshiharu Hata
h: The ceiling lights and lamp fittings
are arranged to create a
centripetal effect and a sense of
direction and depth in this space.

Durch die gemeinsame Anord-
nung der Oberlichter und
Leuchten wird dem Raum Tiefe
und Richtung auf den Mittelpunkt
hin verliehen.

La disposition de l'éclairage du
plafond et des lampes donne à
cet espace une impression de
direction et de profondeur.

i: Floor: carpeting / Walls and
ceiling: vinyl paint / Lamp fittings:
opaque acrylic plate

Boden: Teppich / Wände und
Decke: Vinylfarbe / Leuchten:
undurchsichtige Acryl-Scheiben.

Sol: tapis / Murs et plafond:
peinture en vinyle / Eclairages:
plexiglas opaque.

j: Toshiroh Ikegami Architecture
Company
k: Toshiroh Ikegami Architecture
Company

a: **Toriyama Private Residence**
b: Sakai - shi, Osaka
c: Yoshiko Toriyama
d: Masaki Kishi
e: Masaki Kishi / Katsuya Marutani
f: Kanefuku Sangyo Co., Ltd.
g: Seiichiro Ohtake
h: A variation to the space is afforded by the sense of incompability created by including a grid of fair-faced concrete in the wall structure.

Dieser Raum vermittelt durch die Integration eines Gitters aus Sichtbeton in der Wand den Eindruck von Widersprüchlichkeit.

De par l'inclusion d'une grille de béton apparent dans le mur, cette pièce procure un sentiment de contradiction.
i: Ceiling: soft lysine, silver paint / Walls: soft lysine / Floor: carpet

Decke: Lysine, Silberfarbe / Wände: Lysine / Boden: Teppich

Plafond: tissu suède, peinture argentée / Murs: tissu suède / Sol: tapis.
j: Kishi Masaki + Environment Planning
k: Mosaki Kishi / Kalsuya Marurani

a: **City Screen VII**
b: Mino - shi, Osaka
e: Toshiroh Ikegami and Urban Gauss (Hiroshi Yamaga)
f: Tokuoka Komuten
g: Urban Gauss
h: A living room created by utilizing a mezzanine. The design concept attempts to expand the room optically through a difference in levels, a variation in plane geometry and by concealing the staircase.

Wohnzimmer mit Zwischenetage. Das Ziel des Designs war es, das Wohnzimmer optisch zu vergrößern. Zu diesem Zweck wurden unterschiedliche Ebenen konstruiert und der Treppenaufgang außerhalb des Blickfeldes angelegt.

Salle de séjour en mezzanine. Le but de ce design était d'obtenir un effet optique agrandissant la salle de séjour. C'est la raison pour laquelle différents niveaux ont été construits et que la cage d'escalier n'est pas dans le champ visuel.

i: Floor: tiles, carpet / Walls: fair-faced concrete / Ceiling: excelsior board / Staircase: steel, stainless steel

Boden: Fliesen, Teppich / Wände: Sichtbeton / Decke: Holzwollplatten /Treppe: Stahl, Edelstahl

Sol: carrelage, tapis / Murs: béton apparent / Plafond: plaques de laine de bois / Cage d'escalier: acier, acier spécial

j: Toshiroh Ikegami

a: **House at Nishinomiya**
b: Nishinomiya - shi, Hyogo
c: Kohhei Yoshida
d: Nobuyuki Ishida
e: Nobuyuki Ishida
f: Fujikawa Co., Ltd.
h: Two spaces at different levels
are designed in such a way that
they are made to merge with
each other.

Raum mit zwei ineinander über-
gehenden Ebene.

Pièce à deux niveaux.
i: Floor: Tatami mats, plywood
strips, multicolour paint finish,
exotic timbers / Column: painted
Ceiling: plasterboard + VE

Boden: Tatami-Matten, Sperr-
holzpaneele, mehrfarbiger Anstrich, exotische Hölzer / Säule:
Farbanstrich / Decke: Gipsplatten
und VE

Sol: Tatamis, panneaux en lam-
bris de contre-plaqué, peinture
de plusieurs couleurs, bois
exotiques / Colonnes: peinture /
Plafond: plaques de plâtre et VE
j: ISS Architects Design Office

a: **Hanaoka House**
b: Hiroshima - shi, Hiroshima
c: Fusao Hanaoka
d: Itaru Sasaki
e: Itaru Sasaki
f: Tobishima Construction Co., Ltd.
g: Nishi Nihon Shabo Co., Ltd.:
   Minoru Nakamura
h: The project attempted to amplify living functions by making the elements convey a variety of implications.

   Vielseitig nutzbare Elemente erhöhen die Wohnqualität dieses Raumes.

   De multiples éléments utiles améliorent la qualité d'habitat de cette pièce.
i: Carpet, ceramic tiles, Tatami mats, vinyl cloth, square stainless steel tubes

   Teppich, Keramikfliesen, Tatami-Matten, Vinyltapete, quadratische Röhren aus Edelstahl

   Tapis, carrelage de céramique, Tatamis, tapisserie en vinyle, tubes quadratiques en acier spécial
j: Itaru Sasaki Architects Design Office

a: **Tsuboya no ie**
b: Naha - shi, Okinawa
c: Tsuyoshi Tamai
d: Kazuo Akamine
e: Osamu Senaga
f: Taisin Co., Ltd.
g: Kurihara
h: This residence in Tuboya, a town with a 300-year tradition in eathenware, is built on the site where the ancestor's red brick factory once stood.

Dieses Wohnhaus in Tuboya, einem Dorf mit einer dreihundertjährigen Töpfereitradition, wurde an dem Ort errichtet, wo einst die Ziegelfabrik der Vorfahren der Hausbesitzer gestanden hat. Das Dach des Hauses ist mit Biberziegeln gedeckt.

Cette résidence à Tuboya, une ville d'une tradition en poterie vieille de 300 ans, fut construite sur le site où se trouvait autrefois l'usine de tuiles des ancêtres du propriétaire de l'immeuble. Le toit est couvert de tuiles plates.

i: Fair-faced concrete, plain tiles Ryuku limestone, Apitong wood / Floor: teak

Sichtbeton, Biberziegel, Ryuku-Kalkstein, Apitong-Holz / Boden: Teak

Béton apparent, Apitong-bois / Sol: bois de teck
j: Architects Associate Gan

a. **Sesoil Kawasaki Kyomachi Highrise**
b: Kawasaki - shi, Kanagawa
c: Kowa Real Estate Investment Co., Ltd.
d: Haseko Corporation Co., Ltd.; Hideharu Matsunami
e: Haseko Corporation Co., Ltd.; Junji Kawmura, Mikiko Nagai
f: Haseko Corporation Co., Ltd.
g: Sogei Co., Ltd.
h: In this arrangement, three-dimensional variations are created in the living space with Japanese styling and greenery.

Die Kombination von dreidimensionalen Effekten mit japanischem Styling und Pflanzen unterstreicht das japanische Ambiente des Wohnraums.

La combinaison d'effets à trois dimensions avec le style japonais et les plantes fait ressortir l'atmosphère japonaise de la salle de séjour.

i: Floor: carpet / Walls and ceiling: vinyl cloth / Other elements: Japanese oak, hemlock

Boden: Teppich / Wände und Decke: Vinyltapete / Weitere Baumaterialien: japanische Eiche und Hemlocktanne

Sol: tapis / Murs et plafond: tapisserie en vinyle / Autres matériaux de construction: chêne japonais et cigue
j: Haseko Corporation Co.,Ltd.

a: **Oshika Whaleland**
b: Oshika - cho, Miyagi
c: Oshika cho
d: Art Director: Akihiko Shigyo /
   Designer: Yutaka Uehara /
   Planner: Shinichi Aihara
f: Nomura Co., Ltd.
g: Masami Daito
h: This concept of how a mature
   amusement park should look,
   filled with intellectual pursuits, is
   developed through an atmosphere
   of space, experience and information.

   Durch die Umsetzung der
   Begriffe Raum, Erfahrung und
   Information wurde das Konzept
   eines anspruchsvollen Vergnü-
   gungsparks für Erwachsene
   verwirklicht.

   Grâce à l'interprétation des
   notions espace, expérience et
   information, le concept d'un parc
   d'attractions ambitieux pour
   adultes a été réalisé.
i: Single tubes, steel, planed
   plywood, embossed rubber tiles

   Einzelne Röhren, Stahl, geglät-
   tetes Sperrholz, geprägte
   Gummifliesen

   Tubes uniques, acier, contre-
   plaqué poli, dalle en ciment
   caoutchouté gaufré
j: Nomura Co., Lt

a: **Toyota Automobile Museum**
b: Aichi - gun, Aichi
c: Toyota Motor Corporation
d: Shusaku Nanseki (Nikken Sekkei, Ltd.)
e: Yoshinobu Sato (Nikken Sekkei, Ltd.)
f: Takenaka Corporation
g: Center Photo
h: This is a full-size car museum designed in the form of a flat and rectangular circuit, and an internal atrium spanning the full height of the building.

Museum für Autos. Die ovale Form erinnert an eine Rennbahn. Das Gebäude besitzt einen offenen Innenhof.

Musée de voitures en grandeur originale. La forme ovale rapelle un autodrome. Cour intérieure à ciel ouvert.

i: Floor: carpet tiles / Walls and ceiling: various patterns, sprayed finish

Boden: Teppichfliesen / Wände und Decke: verschiedene Muster, Spritzfarbanstrich

Sol: carrés de tapis / Murs et plafond: différents motifs, peints par pulvérisation

j: Nagoya Office, Nikken Sekkei, Ltd.

a: **Outline**
b: Ogasa - gun, Hamaoka cho,
Sakura, Shizuoka Pref.
Total floor area: 6,672 m²
(exhibition area approx
2,800 m²) Structure: 3 upper
levels and B1 level; height
approx 45 m

Izumi Ban
Kariya Lighting Laboratory
Tomokazu Orikasa
Takahiro Mukai
Youichi Hasegawa
Yukio Koyaide
Gyunichi Toril
Shuichi Kuzi
Mamoru Yazima
Ikuo Takabayashi
Chubu Electric Power Co., Ltd
Morikazu Shibuya
Nikken Sekkei Ltd.
Nomura Display Co., Ltd
Haruaki Sobue
Dentsu Incorporated

a: **Aichi Shukutoku - Gakuen Hida Mountain School Shukuyu - Kan**
b: Mashita - gun, Gifu
c: Aichi Shukutoku Gakuen
e: Takenaka Corporation / Tomio Mitsui, Toshiki Shima
f: Takenaka Corporation
g: Masahiko Tanaka (Photo House Tanaka)

h: A stairwell in the dining room gives the impression of a free and open design concept. The wooden interior of this camping school provides a space filled with nature.

Der Treppenschacht im Eßzimmer zeugt von einem freien, offenen Design-Konzept. Die hölzerne Inneneinrichtung dieser Camping School schafft eine natürliche Umgebung.

La cage d'escalier dans la salle à manger donne une impression de concept de décor libre et ouvert. L'aménagement intérieur en bois de cette école-camping crée un environnement naturel.

i. Exterior: exposed concrete, wood-coloured aluminium strip / Wall, ceiling, handrails: pasted veneer, pine logs

Außenwände: Sichtbeton, holzfarbene Aluminium-Fensterrahmen / Wände, Decke und Geländer: aufgeleimtes Furnier und Kieferblöcke.

Murs extérieurs: béton apparent, châssis de fenêtre en aluminium de couleur bois / Murs, plafond et balustrades: placage collé et rondins de pin

j: Takenaka Corporation

a: **"A Un Tei" Temple´s Institute**

b: Nishinomiya - shi, Hyogo

c: Kannon Temple

e: Nobuyuki Ishida (I.S.S. Architects & Engineers Associates)

f: Tsukimori Komuten Co., Ltd.

g: Nobuyuki Ishida

h: An object can be interpreted as two contrasting extremes in relation to "A Un", such as saintly and common, beginning and end, eternity and instant, continuity and destruction, darkness and brightness, and weight and lightness.

Ein Objekt kann als Symbol zweier gegensätzlicher Extreme im Sinne von „A Un" angesehen werden und spiegelt den Kontrast von heilig und profan, Anfang und Ende, Ewigkeit und Jetzt, Kontinuität und Zerstörung, Dunkelheit und Licht, Schwere und Leichtigkeit wider.

Un objet peut être considéré comme symbole de deux extrêmes opposés dans le sens de «A Un» et réflète le contraste de sacré et profane, début et fin, éternité et moment, continuité et destruction, obscurité et lumière, poids et légèreté.

i: Floor: Tatami mats, framed plywood / Walls: plasterboard / Ceiling: plasterboard + VE

Boden: Tatami-Matten, Sperrholzrahmen / Wände: Gipsplatten / Decke: Gipsplatten und VE

Sol: Tatamis, châssis en contreplaqué / Murs: plaques de plâtre / Plafond: plaques de plâtre et VE

j: I.S.S. Architects & Engineers Associates

a: **Kobe Port Island Hall (World Hall) Kobe Port Island Sports Center**
b: Kobe - shi, Hyogo
c: Kobe - shi
e: Kobe - shi / Shiro Mitsumune / Sumio Mimura / Kinzo Tsuchiya Yoshihisa Uchida
f: Takenaka Komuten / Kajima Corporation
g: Shiro Shuda / Kazuo Natori

h: An interior that establishes a synergic effect of design, dynamics, lighting and sound, and so creates coherence with the external appearance. A pair of buildings that are in symmetric harmony.

Das Zusammenwirken von Design, Dynamik, Beleuchtung und Klang zeichnet das Innere des Gebäudes aus und schafft auf diese Weise eine Einheit von innerer und äußerer Gestaltung. Die beiden Gebäude befinden sich im perfekten Einklang.

L'effet combiné du décor, de la dynamique, de l'éclairage et du son fait ressortir l'intérieur du bâtiment et crée de cette façon un unité dans la décoration intérieure. Les deux bâtiments se trouvent en parfaite harmonie.

i: Weatherproof steel sheeting / brick tiles / flooring / glass wool boards

Wetterfeste Stahlbleche, Backsteinfliesen, Fußboden, Platten aus Glaswolle

Planche en acier résistant aux intempériers, briques, revêtement, plaques de laine de verre

j: Showa Sekkei

a: **Mukogawa Senior High School, Junior High School Pool**
b: Nishinomiya - shi, Hyogo
c: Mukogawa Gakuin
d: Takenaka Corporation/ Kunihiko Honjo, Yasuo Mokutani
f: Takenaka Corporation
g: Yuji Takahashi
h: Japan's first medium-sized sliding roof. We adopted a shell structure with a rotating, folding fan, and tried to produce a graceful appearence.

Das erste Schiebedach mittlerer Größe in Japan. Man entschied sich für einen muschelförmigen Bau mit einem beweglichen, fächerförmigen Faltdach. Ein elegantes Aussehen stand im Vordergrund.

Le premier toit ouvrant de taille moyenne au Japon. Une construction en forme de coquille avec un toit plissé mobile en éventail a été adoptée.

i: Roof and ceiling: PVC membrane / Pool and surrounds: ceramic tiles

Dach und Decke: PVC-Membran / Schwimmbecken und Schwimmbadbereich: Keramikfliesen

Toit et plafond: membrane / PVC / Bassin et toute la piscine: carrelage de céramique

j: Takenaka Corporation

a: **Logos Church**
b: Hachioji - shi, Tokyo
c: Logos Church
e: GK Sekkei Associates
f: Taisei Corporation
g: Gantame
h: The Cross on the flat roof at the top of the fan-shaped plan reflects the change of the sky against the wooden background. Closing the windows causes the interior to take on the role of a multipurpose space.

Das Kreuz auf dem Flachdach an der Spitze des fächerförmigen Grundrisses reflektiert gegen den Holzhintergrund jede Veränderung des Himmels. Wenn man die Fenster schließt, wird das Innere des Gebäudes zu einem multifunktionalen Raum.

La croix sur le toit plat en haut du plan en éventail reflète sur l'arrière-plan du bois chaque variation dans le ciel. Lorsque l'on ferme les fenêtres, l'intérieur du bâtiment se transforme en espace multifonctionnel.

i: Ceiling: EP spraying on board / Wall: fair-faced RC / Floor: carpet

Decke: Platten mit EP-Spritz-farbabstrich / Wände: Sicht-stahlbeton / Fußboden: Teppich

Plafond: plaques peintes en EP par pulvérisation / Murs: béton armé apparent / Sol: tapis
j: GK Sekkei Associates

a: **Hasegawa Art Museum**
b: Setagaya - ku, Tokyo
c: Hasegawa Art Museum
d: Tsuyoshi Fukumoto
e: Tsuyoshi Fukumoto / Teiichi Nishikawa
f: Kajima Corporation
g: Akiko Kawasumi
h: A museum for the exhibition of pictures and ceramic ware collected by Miss Machiko Hasegawa including her "Sazaesan" works.

Museum, in dem die Gemälde- und Keramiksammlung von Frau Machiko Hasegawa sowie ihre Arbeiten mit dem Titel „Sazaesan" zu besichtigen sind.

Musée, dans lequel on peut admirer une exposition de tableaux et de faïences, collectionnés par Madame Machiko Hasegawa, ainsi que ses travaux portant le titre «Sazaesan».

i: Brick, natural linoleum, glass, glass cloth, cherry wood plywood

Mauerstein, Linoleum, Glas, Glasfaser, Sperrholz mit Kirschbaumfurnier

Brique, linoléum, verre, fibre de verre, contre-plaqué en cerisier
j: KAJIMA DESIGN (Kajima Corporation Architectural and Engineering Design Group)
k: Kajima Corporation

a: **Wakita Museum of Art**
b: Kita - Saku - gun, Nagoya
c: Juridical Foundation Wakita Museum of Art
d: Basic Planning: Kazu Wakita / Architectural Design & Interior Design: Hidefumi Suzuki, Katsumi Kosuge (KAJIMA DESIGN) / Interior Design & Monument: Studio A, Aijiro Wakita
f: Kajima Corporation, Kanto Branch
g: Hiroshi Ueda (Shin Kenchiku - sha)
h: Mild lights pierce through delicately cut apertures. The exhibition space was designed for various dialogues with the environment.

Die eingebauten Lampen tauchen den Raum in ein sanftes Licht. Der Ausstellungsraum lädt zum Dialog ein.

Les lumières incorporées plongent la pièce dans une lumière tamisée. L'espace d'exposition invite au dialogue.

i: Floor: polished marble / Walls: AEP covered with glass cloth / Ceiling: AEP

Boden: Polierter Marmor / Wände: AEP mit Glasfaserüberzug / Decke: AEP

Sol: marbre poli / Murs: AEP recouverts de fibre de verre / Plafond: AEP
j: KAJIMA DESIGN (Kajima Corporation Architectural and Engineering Design Group)

a: **Itoki Ginza Gallery - Life Stage**
b: Chuo - ku, Tokyo
c: Itoki Co., Ltd.
d: AD & A, Tetsuo Komada, Yoko Takemura
f: Naigai Mokuzai Kogyo
g: Minoru Karamatsu (Karamatsu Photo Office)
h: A gallery space comprising a gate, a tube and an exhibition hall which forms the entrance to another dimension far removed from the bustle of Ginza.

Galerieraum mit einem Torbogen und einer Röhre. Die Ausstellungshalle wirkt wie das Tor zu einer anderen Welt fernab von der Hektik Ginzas.

Galerie avec des arceaux, des tubes et un hall d'exposition. Elle semble être la porte sur un autre monde, loin du tumulte de Ginza.

i: Ediaruta-quartzite, pickled steel plate (joripato), coloured urerthane glaze

Ediaruta-Quarzit, gebeiztes Stahlblech (Joripato), farbig glasiertes Urethan

Quartzite Ediaruta, planche d'acier décapé (joripato), uréthane veris en couleur

j: AD & A Inc.

a: **Itoki Ginza Gallery -
   Presentation Salon**
b: Chuo - ku, Tokyo
c: Itoki Co., Ltd
d: AD & A, Tetsuo Komada, Yoko
   Takemura
f: Naigai Mokuzai Kogyo
g: Minoru Karamatsu (Karamatsu
   Photo Office)
h: A saloon of dramatic structure
   equipped with AV equipment and
   a stepped floor, which can also
   be used for presentation
   purposes.

   Ein bühnenartiger Salon mit
   Audio-Videoausrüstung und
   einem Podium, das auch für
   Aufführungen genutzt werden
   kann.

   Un salon avec une structure
   semblable à celle d'un théâtre
   avec un équipement audio-visuel
   et un podium, pouvant servir pour
   des représentations.

i: Flooring, removable carpet,
   floored with vinyl cloth

   Fußboden, runder Teppich,
   Unterseite Vinylgewebe

   Revêtement, tapis rond, dessous
   en tissu vinyle
j: AD & A Inc.